How To Get Rich Without Working

by Edward Homer Bailey.

with an introduction by Roger Chambers

Self Reliance Books

Get more historic titles on animal and stock breeding, gardening and old fashioned skills by visiting us at:

http://selfreliancebooks.blogspot.com/

Introduction

I am pleased to present yet another title in our "How To ..." series.

The work is in the Public Domain and is re-printed here in accordance with Federal Laws.

As with all reprinted books of this age that are intended to perfectly reproduce the original edition, considerable pains and effort had to be undertaken to correct fading and sometimes outright damage to existing proofs of this title. At times, this task is quite monumental, requiring an almost total "rebuilding" of some pages from digital proofs of multiple copies. Despite this, imperfections still sometimes exist in the final proof and may detract from the visual appearance of the text.

I hope you enjoy reading this book as much as I enjoyed making it available to readers again.

Roger Chambers

No good book fulfills its purpose unless it is read by as many as possible. Pass this along to a friend. We will send you other literature, if you want it.

How to Get Rich Without Working

BY EDWARD HOMER BAILEY

I had been a reporter for The Times for over twelve years. I began work on the paper as "devil", my duties being to dust the office furniture, clean the spittoons, attend the fires when fires were needed, carry the mail, run errands and make myself generally useful. At the end of three years, during which time I drew a salary of $1 per week or $52 annually, I was told by Mr. Bishop, the editor and proprietor of The Times that I had earned promotion, that he had employed another boy to serve as "devil," and that I should have a "case" and a chance to become a full-fledged printer. I thanked him for his consideration of me, but not in words that conveyed to him anything like the depth of my gratitude. I cannot recall a happier day than that on which I enjoyed the distinction of being promoted from office boy to printer. At once I entered upon my new duties with a determination and ambition that must have gratified Mr. Bishop, for one day he came to me and said:

"Sammy, one of these days you will be a reporter. You show an attention to detail in following copy that convinces me that you are cut out for a newspaper man; so I want you to stick to the case for three or four years, learn all you can, get punctuation, capitalization, grammar, and all that sort of thing down fine, and then come to me and I will see if I cannot give you a job hustling for news."

One day in the summer of 1888, after I had mastered the art of type-sticking, I hung my coat on a peg in the editorial room. "Coal Oil Charley" peered at me from his case in the news room. "Old Soak", who was the swiftest type-setter in the shop and whose thirst for liquor he regarded as one of the blessings of his life, gave me a stare that indicated that Mr. Bishop would be sorry that he picked me from the case to send me out as a reporter. I could plainly see that all the printers in the composing room were disposed to "give me the laugh," as the phraseology of the street goes. However, my coat was hung on the peg—not because that was part of the duty of a reporter, but because the weather was hot, in evidence of which Mr. Bishop himself was in his shirt sleeves, all windows were up, the printers were working with their suspenders down, and the exchange editor was mopping perspiration from his brow.

It is the strangest thing in all my career as a newspaper reporter that my first reportorial contribution to The Times was the most notable, romantic and important that I have any recollection of; and yet the part I played in it was small. I was merely the machine through which it was shaped and put into "copy." I did not even "discover" the man from whom I obtained my topic and I did not realize until after my article appeared in print that it contained a remarkable truth that the whole world seemed to have lost sight of. For years since its appearance I have covered the whole field of journalism, from writing small personals, weddings, parties, accidents and deaths, to the great national conventions of the various political parties, including interviews with many of the most distinguished men of this country and Europe, but in all this time I have not eclipsed my first day's work, though it may be true that I gained what credit I have earned in my profession wholly as a result of the mass of stuff I have written for The Times since the event of which I speak.

Having placed my coat on the peg and felt uneasy under the stare of "Coal Oil Charley" and "Old Soak," I took a seat at the desk which Mr. Bishop had advised me should be my permanent place to work. I busied myself getting books and news-papers in order, wondering all the while how I should begin to grind out "copy" for printers whom I knew would soon be hungry for it. I was not long in doubt, however, as to what my first step should be. Mr. Bishop came to my desk and said: "Here is a letter from a man who is evidently crazy. He used to live here. I knew him when he was the laziest boy in town. He went away years ago way out to Chicago, when that place was not much larger than a minute and located in a sickly swamp at that. He says he is back here to take a rest and enjoy the scenes of his childhood. Rest is good. If he has ever worked a day since he left here and is tired now, that would be news worth publishing in this town. Here read this letter and then go and see if he isn't crazy."

Mr. Bishop tossed a letter to my desk and I read:

My Dear Mr. Bishop: I am here on a visit to the scenes of my childhood and incidentally to take a rest. You will doubtless remember when I was a boy here, too contrary to go to school; that I went away one day and finally turned up in Chicago. Since that time, you know, the aunt with whom I was living here, has been buried now over twenty years, I believe. While I am here I am going to erect a big monument over her grave. She deserves the best I can secure, for I am a millionaire now and I owe every cent of it to her. If you can send a reporter to my rooms in the hotel I can tell him a story to fill up the paper with. I can tell him how to get rich without working, just as I did. I want all my hardworking friends here to know how simple a thing it is to amass a great fortune without doing a single day's work. Do not believe I am jesting.

Yours truly,

July 18, 1878.   GEORGE ARCHIE BOWEN.

I read the letter over and over, and was in much doubt as to the character of the man. But I hurriedly slipped on my coat, though I would rather have gone in my shirt sleeves, so oppressively hot was the day. Jogging along toward the Le Grande Hotel I drew a mental picture of the man for whom I was in quest. "Too contrary to go to school," he said in his letter, yet evidently he had gone to school, for he could write cleverly. Maybe he had graduated at a college since locating in Chicago; but how in the world, I wondered, did he become a millionaire without working! That was a puzzling question to me and I was about to assure myself that Geroge Archie Bowen was a wild lunatic when the clerk at the Le Grande Hotel tapped the bell for the boy to show me to "Room 20"

"Well, whoever he is," said I to myself, as the elevator shot upwards, "he is occupying the finest quarters in this place, and maybe if he is crazy he is not dangerous; for," I continued to reason, "they would not harbor dangerous lunatics in this house."

"Come in, come in," came cheerily from the inside as I lightly rapped on the door of Room 20. I hesitated about doing so, a fear having suddenly seized me that the man might be at that very moment pointing a bulldog revolver at the door ready to shoot as soon as it should open; but "Come in" from the voice once more reassured me and I walked into the presence of a sweltering stranger.

"Samuel T. Essington," he said, glancing at the card I had previously sent him

and advancing with outstretched hand.
"I am glad to see you; yes indeed, I am
very glad to see you. I like newspaper
men; always did like newspaper men.
Hot—ain't it? Well, hot is no name for
it. Actually, I am done—done enough
right now to carve on the table. Just look
at the sauce on me. I'm boiling all over.
Here, have a chair. Move it over to that
window."

While George Archie Bowen thus chatted
and made me feel at ease all at once, I was
making up my mind that I was in the
presence of a jolly, good-natured, fine-look-
ing gentleman. He had a face that was full
of fresh bloom, as plump and smooth as
a baby's and bright blue eyes that sparkled
with good humor. "Laughing George"
was the name I mentally gave him before
I had been in his presence a minute. I
observed that his hands were as pretty as a
woman's and at once connected this fact
with his letter in which he said something
about how to get rich without working.
He was plainly, though stylishly dressed. A
diamond sparkled in a milk white shirt front
and a very dainty fob dangled beneath his
vest. He did not look over fifty years old,
though there was a large, glossy, cheerful
stretch of baldness on a well developed
head. There was something in the bald
spot which seemed to inspire confidence in
the man. It appeared to be looking right
at me like an old and good friend and I
felt at home in its presence in spite of the
forebodings of a few moments before.

"Why," said Mr. Bowen, as I took a seat at the window and had not yet been given an opportunity to thank him for his cordial welcome. "I used to know a Samuel T. Essington in this town. That was your father, I guess. That was when I was a mere stripling. He was as old then as I am now, and I guess he is dead before this. He was a mighty good man. I can remember that he was a great church-goer and people around here said he was the best blacksmith in the whole country. So you are Samuel T. Essington, Jr. ?"

I attempted to stammer out that he had guessed it right, but he evidently did not take note of my embarrassment, for he continued chatting pleasantly.

"Well, now, Sammy," he said, "There isn't a man in all this town more welcome than you are. As I said before, I like the company of newspaper men, and I make no distinction among them. You are a reporter for The Times?"

"Yes, sir," I replied with as much politeness as I could command.

"Well, you know, I wrote a note to Bishop telling him I was in town and requesting him to send a reporter up here. I don't mind telling you that I was sure Bishop himself would come, for Bishop and I used to be boys together long years ago, and I thought of course he would be glad to see me. I—I—beg pardon."

I was about to interrupt Mr. Bowen with the remark that Mr. Bishop thought the author of the note a lunatic, but I caught my tongue in time and merely said:

"He was busy and sent me."

"That was just right. Don't think for a minute that you are not just as welcome here as Mr. Bishop would be. Mr. Bishop may come any time, but I'll save him the trouble of making the first call by going to see him before the week is over. I don't know many people here any more. I used to know all of them. My! how the old town has grown! The old mill is about the only familiar spot I have been able to locate. That looks older than it did, and it ought to, for it was old and full of rats when I used to play in it. Old Justice Hogue is still running his little pill shop and paper stand, I see, only he is in a new building—that is, the building is new to me, because it was not there when I left the town. Well, Squire Hogue will die here yet. Seems to me he has been here twice as long as the town. What's become of Sallie Sallee?"

"I never knew her," I replied. "However, I know of her. She married a farmer's son—a fellow named Ed Shy—and they're living somewhere in the country. Doing pretty well, I guess," I added.

"Glad to hear it. Very glad to hear it. Sallie used to be a chum of mine and many is the time I've kissed her at the parties we youngsters used to have at the neighbors' in the old days. I wouldn't know her now if she were to step right in this room. And there was Jimmy O'Donnell. What in the world has become of Jimmy? He was a corker when I knew him. He—"

"Jimmy," said I, interrupting, "is an ex-member of the legislature. He is living here in retirement in his old age."

"Good. I will have to hunt Jimmy up. I'll send him a note before to-morrow. We used to be as thick as low boiled, and played marbles and went swimming to-together. And Clarence Safford—what has become of him?"

"I believe he is married and living in St. Louis."

"Well, I am sorry I didn't know that. I have often gone from Chicago to St. Louis, but never happened to run across him. Wouldn't known him, I guess, if I had. But he was a monkey when he was a boy! I'll never forget his tricks on the boys when we used to play 'grab' in the barns, and when we used to play 'hole in the ground.' He was the worst mischief-maker in this whole countryful of boys around here. I never will forget how he used to catch innocent little dogs and put turpentine"—

It was manifest that Mr. Bowen had not dwelt on the fact that I was a business and not a social guest, and when I pulled out my watch to note the time and perhaps at the same time gave evidence of entertaining a fear that I was remaining away from the office too long, he halted in his reminiscences, taking a hint that I had not intended to convey.

"Pardon me, Mr. Essington," he said, pulling out his own watch. "I am always forgetting that time flies. You came here in response to my note to Mr. Bishop and I should not have bored you with my reminiscences.

"No offense, I am sure," I politely replied.

"But I have needlessly detained you. The fact is I should like to detain you for some time yet, for I want to tell you something that is as strange as anything you ever heard in your life. It is a long story and some way I feel that the world ought to know it. The story has never been told —not to a living soul—and if The Times publishes it, it will be a 'scoop.' I'll tell you what I'll do: I'll send a note to Bishop asking him to allow you to spend the day with me and begging him to excuse you from the office to-day."

Mr. Bowen was about to ring the call bell for a boy, when I interrupted.

"Let me write the note. I know how to arrange it," and I proceeded to scratch off a few lines in my note book. Mr. Bowen pulled the bell, a boy came and he was off with my message. I was sure this was a good stroke, for a note from Mr. Bowen, urging my presence with him all day, would have convinced Mr. Bishop beyond all doubt that Bowen was really insane; that I would know it and promptly return to the office. This was all I wrote Bishop:

"Bowen is not insane. He is a fine,

bright fellow and he has a great story to tell me. I will not get through with him until late this evening. Don't expect me."

And this message came back.

"All right. Work up his story for all it is worth.   BISHOP."

II.

"Some men," said Mr. Bowen, vigorously fanning himself and adjusting a handkerchief about his sweltering neck, "have grown rich by very hard work; others by embezzling public and private funds; others by accepting bribes and others by stage and other arts; but few rich men, if any, have amassed millions through these avenues. Being a millionaire myself, I know just exactly how millionaires obtain their fabulous wealth. You are here to get my story of how to get rich without out working. It is not by stealing or ways of trickery. That is the reason my story will interest you and the readers of The Times.

"I have passed the meridian of life," continued Mr. Bowen, "and I say to you upon my honor as a gentleman that I possess a fortune aggregating $50,000,000 and that I have never worked a day in my life to earn a dollar of it—not a single dollar. But I did obtain every cent of it legally and all the world could not honestly take one cent of it from me. When I say that I nave never worked a day in my life, I mean to say that I have never engaged in actual effort to earn a dollar by the sweat of my brow."

Pausing a moment as if anticipating that I might leave my notes long enough to interject a remark to the effect that "by the sweat of thy brow thou shalt eat bread," Mr. Bowen proceeded.

"Never mind that old Bible quotation. I know all about that. I say I have never earned a single dollar by the sweat of my brow, but all my vast wealth I obtained legally, strictly according to the laws of the land; strictly in accordance with the rules and by the sanction of the courts; by means practiced and upheld by the church, by the press, by business men, by the president of the United States, by your senates and congresses, by your legislatures, by your governors, by your county and city authorities. That's why I say, never mind that old Bible quotation. If I have never earned a single dollar by the sweat of my brow, your preachers, your churches, and your Christian people can't point their fingers in scorn at me. The means by which I have become so enormously rich are believed by them to be right and just; they sustain and defend the system that has enabled me to grow rich without working, and why, then, should I be ashamed to tell my story to the world? Let it be made plain in The Times—that I have obtained every dollar of my vast wealth legally and in accordance with what the courts, the churches and the people hold to be just, but not a single dollar of it by the sweat of my brow."

Mr. Bowen left his chair at the window paced across the room once or twice, eyed me closely and appeared a bit excited.

"Is that clear, Mr. Essington?" he inquired.

"That seems to me as clear as a bell, Mr. Bowen," I replied, perhaps with a puzzled look in my face.

"I see that I've got you guessing," he laughed.

"How do you mean?" I asked.

"Why you are wondering, of course, how in the name of goodness I became a millionaire legally without working. That's just as plain in your face as that hot sun over this earth is."

I admitted that something of that kind was on my mind.

"Of course; I knew it," said Mr. Bowen, "and they'll be guessing before they get through reading my story in The Times. Now let me tell," he proceeded, after resuming his chair at the window and again applying the fan, "I was born in this town. I don't remember anything about my mother. She died when I was an infant; and then my father died when I was about six years old. I was the only child. My aunt, my father's sister, was my only relative. She was never married, but she had a little home of her own here and she took me to live with her. She kept a small garden patch, had three cows, some pigs and raised lots of chickens. She got along in life very comfortably somehow. She sold milk and butter and eggs and garden stuff to her neighbors and earned what I suppose some people call a good living. I was her pet. She must have loved me like a mother. She would never allow me to work. She said she wanted to give me a good education and she sent me to school. I liked the school room for a while but it finally grew monotonous and I put in the time playing. I won't stop to tell you how Safford and I played circus and pursued other amusements. We had a glorious childhood life of it, anyway. My aunt humored me. When I didn't want to go to school she did not scold me. She would simply hug and kiss me and say, 'Auntie is awfully sorry,' and then she would tell me to run along and play, 'and maybe you will be good some day and go to school,' she would say.

"But I didn't. I just fooled along until one day an impulse to go west and live with the Indians seized me. I don't know how long I traveled, nor how many miles, but I enjoyed the trip, for it was easy in those days to get along. I never had to go hungry nor without a good bed. The farmers always seemed glad to see me and had lots of questions to ask me. I finally found myself in a small lumber camp near what is now the site of Chicago. I didn't think about asking anybody for work. I was welcome in the camp and had all I wanted to eat. One day a letter came to me from old 'Squire Hogue. He said my aunt was dead and had left me her little home. She had died, he said, of a broken heart because I had left her. He wanted to know what to do about the property. I wrote and told him to sell it and send me the money. Several months later—I had forgotten all about the matter—Old 'Squire Hogue wrote me stating that he had $150 he would send me if I would tell him where to send it. Two weeks later the money came into my hands. It was the sum total of my aunt's bequest, after paying her funeral and necessary court expenses incident to the transfer of the property. I bought a few clothes, treated the boys in camp and had $137 left. It was too much money for me. I wondered what I should do with it.

"Why not buy some land near Chicago," said Charley Neeld, a big lumberman who was for years afterwards my protector and defender.

"'What! Swamp land!" said I.

"'Certainly,' said he.

"'What could I do with it?'

"'Just simply put your money in it until you get ready to leave,' said he.

"I bought 12 acres at $10 an acre two miles from Old Fort Dearborn, and it was a sickly-looking waste at that. I didn't think much about it until one day a fellow came to me and said:

"'What'll you take for them 12 acres?'

"'Don't want to sell,' said I.

"'Why?

"'Just don't want to sell, that's all.'

"'How much did it cost ye?

"'O, just $120,' said I.

"'I'll give you $220 for it,' said he.

"'But I don't want to sell.'

"'I'll give ye $320 for it then.'

"'What's that?' shouted Neeld, who was present.

"'Why,' said the stranger, 'I'll give this here young feller $320 fer them 12 acres ver yonder.'

"'Take it Archie,' said Neeld. 'You can buy a bigger piece.'

"I took Neeld's advice, sold the twelve acres and then looked around for a re-investment. I found five acres nearer the town that a fellow wanted $50 an acre for. I bought it and paid the cash and had $70 left. I divided with Neeld, and for a year had forgotten all about my land until a lawyer in Chicago wrote me saying he had a client who had taken a fancy to my plot. Chicago by this time had increased several hundred in population and it was growing towards my piece. Still I didn't think anything about that, but the recollection of $200 profit on my first deal inspired me to call on the lawyer in Chicago. He seemed mighty glad to see me and said right at once that he would give me $625 for my land.

"'It's worth it,' I said.

"'Will you take it?' he inquired.

"'I guess I will—strictly cash.'

"'O, certainly, all the money is ready.'

"After making the deal I took a little walk around the town, wondering what I should do next. I stepped into a little shoe shop to have some pegs put into my boot heels and while I was waiting for the shoemaker to finish the job I was interested in an inquiry he made.

"'Don't know nobody around here that wants to buy a lot, do ye?'

"'Where's the lot?'

"'This'n right here.'

"'Who owns it?'

"'I do.'

"'This building too?'

"'Yep, sir.'

"'How much do you want for it?' I inquired.

"'Well, not much. You see, I'm no good in this climate. I've got to git out. Doing fine though, but I can't stand this wind here. Doctor says I must go sommers else. If you knows as anybody that wants to buy, I'll sell this whole shootin' match for just what it cost me.'

"'How much is that?'

"'I paid $150 for the lot and put up the building myself. And the building cost me $235.'

"'I'll take it,' said I, and I counted out $385. 'Here's your money; fix the deed.'

"I joined Neeld at the camp with $240 in my pocket more than I had when I started. I made Neeld a present of $100 of it.

"'Say,' said Neeld, 'what'll I do with this money?'

"'Go and buy some land,' said I.

"Neeld laughed. 'I guess I'll send

some of it home to my mother,' he remarked.

*   *   *   *   *   *   *   *

"Six months later I went to Chicago to
see the man who had been occupying my
building for three months. He was con-
ducting a general store in it and was making money. He paid me three months'
rent—$30—and said he would like to buy
the place if I would sell.

"'Guess I won't sell,' I told him. 'But
I will rent to you for another year and
guarantee that no one else shall get it in
that time.'

"This proposition suited him, but he
said to bind the bargain he would pay the
year in advance. I agreed and he handed
over $120, in return for which I gave him
a receipt in full for one year's rental and a
written pledge that I would not sell the
property before the expiration of the time.
So I walked out of the store with $150 of
his money in my pocket, and as I sauntered
along I wondered what a real snap I had.
There was a lot, I thought, for which I had
no earthly use and to the value of which
I had not contributed one single cent, yet I
was able without any effort on my part, to
take from the earnings of the grocer $150
for the privilege of occupying my land. I
had his money right in my pocket and it
struck me as strange that I should have it.
' And besides,' I thought to myself, 'I still
possess the house and lot, and yet he has

paid me to-day almost as much for the use of the lot as I originally paid for it myself:

———

III.

"Here," said Mr. Bowen, reaching in his hip pocket, producing a small, flat leather case and extracting from it a piece of paper yellow with age, "is the next chapter. Read that."

I turned it over and over. It was a clipping from a newspaper, but there was nothing in it or on either side of it, to indicate from what paper it had been cut nor when it had been printed, and I glanced inquiringly at Mr. Bowen.

"The day following the payment of the $150 rent to me by the storekeeper one of the lumbermen brought a copy of the Chicago Gazette out to camp. It was in that paper I found the article you hold in your hand."

Upon one side of it were incomplete parts of advertisments and on the other was this :

RAILROAD COMING.

The Gazette is glad to inform its readers that the Illinois Central Railroad Corporation is turning dirt and will build a railroad into Chicago along the route surveyed two years ago. Several hundred men and teams have been put to work grading and the president of the corporation informs us that work will not stop until the steam horse is running into Chicago. He says that Chicago will soon be a city and that there is no doubt that the road will pay a profit on the money invested. This is certainly good news to Chicago property holders, for the building of a railroad to this place will enhance the value of their land. Every taxpayer ought to encourage the enterprise, because it means a boom. Land is already much higher than it was before the railroad was surveyed and now that work on it has commenced a sharp advance has been noted, especially along the route surveyed. Property that sold a month ago for $100 an acre cannot be bought now for $300 an acre. Besides the building of the railroad, population has increased wonderfully during the past year and in another year we confidently expect to double the number of our inhabitants.

———

After I had concluded reading and making a note of the foregoing, I handed it to Mr. Bowen with the remark:

"The Gazette was a pretty good prophet, wasn't it?"

"Better than it knew," Mr. Bowen responded. "Things went on a boom at once and the way Chicago grew surprised the whole world! It grew so fast that one could not keep track of it. Before the year was up with the storekeeper he offered me $4,000 for my house and lot, but I conuded to hold on to it. On the day his ase expired he was so eager to buy the place that he offered me $4,200 for it, but I realized that it would pay me to hold onto it.   He was very much put out because I would not sell at any price, but he was happy two weeks later when he showed me a deed for the vacant lot adjoining the one which I had refused to sell him.

"'I paid $4,500 for it,' he said, 'because I have built up a large and profitable trade here and I might lose it if I should locate somewhere else.   I am going to build a large two-story house on it at once and put in a big stock of dry goods and boots and shoes and live upstairs with my family. So I want to rent your place until I can build.   How much rent do you want?'

"'Well, the property is worth more than it was,' said I 'and I ought to charge you more than $10 a month.'

" 'Why should you charge me more?' the merchant inquired.

"'Simply because the property has increased in value,' I explained.

" 'Well, I don't deny that,' he replied; 'but you see your investment is no larger than it was a year ago, and you have added no improvements to the building.   And the increased value is not the result of any effort you have made, because you have not done a thing.

" 'I know that,' said I, 'but you can't blame me for getting all the rent I can.   I can rent it to another party who wants to start a grocery store for more than you are paying me and I would not be justified in renting it to you for less than he would be willing to pay.'

"'How much is that?' the shopman asked.

"'Fifteen dollars a month.'

"'Well,' said he, after a moment's reflection, 'if you will rent it to me for another four months I will pay you that much.'

"I agreed to the proposition and received the rent in advance—$60—and as I had now nearly $150 surplus cash on hand and a pretty sure thing so far as income from property was concerned, I felt that I should like to find an opportunity to invest at least $100 of my surplus.

"After weeks of scheming I conceived the idea of forming a land syndicate. I interested a number of friends in it. I pointed out to them the fact that a railroad was coming and that the time to buy was before the railroad arrived, even at any price, for whatever we should pay we could sell at a higher figure after the railroad should come in. My friends had confidence in me, for all of them knew that I had been lucky. The upshot of it was that eighteen of us pooled our issues, raised $100 each and with the $1,800 bought one acre of ground adjoining Fort Dearborn for $9,000, executing a mortgage for deferred payments.

"This investment," continued Mr. Bowen, "proved a little bonanza. A large portion of it was leased to parties who at once erected business houses upon it. The leases in every instance, were for five years, with the privilege of purchase at valuation at the expiration of that time or a re-lease for a period of 15 years on the revaluation. How much do you think the syndicate made the first five years?"

"Can't guess," said I.

"Well," Mr. Bowen slowly resumed, "as a matter of fact the syndicate did not earn a cent, for it did nothing but take from the occupants of the one acre all in the form of rent that it could extract. There were, I say eighteen of us in the syndicate, and the $7,200 balance we owed as the purchase price we realized the first two years from rent, so that, if you look at it right, the syndicate made the occupants of the ground —the business men—pay for the property. The syndicate was never out but $1,800—but it even got the $1,800 back and at the expiration of the first five years not only put back into its pocket the original $1,800 it invested, but the record showed that five years' rent to the men who did business netted an actual profit, after paying a debt of $7,200 and interest, of something over $17,000—nearly $1,000 each for eighteen people.

The statement just concluded startled me, and Mr. Bowen observed the fact.

"I tell you, Mr. Essington, that is only the small end of the deal. You see, after all, the syndicate did not buy that land! The men who occupied it—the men who had the use of it and employed labor upon it and helped keep the world moving—paid for it twice over and yet didn't own a foot of it. We, the syndicate, that did not buy it but had the deed for it and the power to charge rent, still owned it, so that when the five-year leases were up—why, there the syndicate stood, not only ready but with legal power to make the occupants BUY the land a few times more.

"Well, Chicago was growing wonderfully and demand for business sites was sharply increasing. The men on the syndicate land wanted to stay. Some concluded to buy. Three parties paid $10,000 each for a lot, only a little total of $30,000 for less than half an acre. The other tenants re-leased for fifteen years on the re-valuation giving us a steady annual income."

"That's certainly a sure way to get rich without working," I ventured to say.

"Only scheme in the world that is legal ; that is justified by our courts and our legislative powers; that is upheld by the church, sustained by the great clergy and the powerful press. People who get rich without working in any other way are thieves or gamblers. The man who speculates in wheat on the board of trade is denounced by press and pulpit as an enemy to society; and the man who sits at a card table and bets money on a poker hand is regarded as only one step from the Devil. Yet after all; the grain speculator and the card player, while it is true are dangerous to society, have nothing like the power the landlord has to extract money from the pockets of the people. You sit down to a card table with a gambler.   He allows you to deal, and affords you every opportunity to see that the game shall be square, with the result that he fails to 'freeze you out,' and you play along with him with equal chances of winning.   But there is only one dealer when it comes to the land—he is the landlord.   If the landlord says, 'Fork over $1,000,' that is just what you must pay or get off the earth.   If the landlord says, 'I must take from you $5,000, $10,000, $20,000, $50,000, $100,000, $1,000,000,' you have but one alternative ; you must pay or get off.   You have no chance to deal. You are in the game only to the extent that you must pay as the landlord directs and demands."

"Can't a man leave the game with the landlord and go somewhere else ?"

"Yes," Mr. Bowen smiled.   "If one is not a land owner and wants to escape the landlord's game he can go jump into the river and end his existence.   Every man who is not a land owner must play with the landlord, upon the terms of the landlord, according to the rules of the game of the landlord, and if he will not so play, he must go jump off, that's all."

IV.

Mr. Bowen's revelations in the foregoing chapter were startling to me.   The power that some men have to grow unusually rich, apparently without effort, was as clear to me now as the noon-day sun.   I saw at

once where the "genius" of the Astors
came in ; how it was possible for them to
astound the world with their display of
wealth ; how, after all, the property which
they "own" was never paid for by them,
but was bought many times over by the
tenants, and how the Astors were able to
live like kings in Europe upon the sweat
of the brow of labor.   But I was not pre-
pared when Mr. Bowen closely followed
with another revelation of the power of the
landlord.   I had only seen part of the
claws of the man who plays a "dead sure
game."   Taking up the chain of his story
where he left off, Mr. Bowen continued :

"That the syndicate had made a fortune
without effort or expenditure of money be-
longing to it was fully understood by me
and my friends.   We still owned more
than half the Fort Dearborn property and
from this we were able upon a re-valuation,
to fix an annual rental of $6,000 for a
period of fifteen years, at the end of which
time the leases were to expire and the property, if wanted, to be sold to occupants
at present valuation.

"In the meantime, however, I was looking after my property which the storekeeper had occupied.   He had long since
vacated my premises and was doing business alongside in his own house and on his
own land.   But I was not without a tenant.
A cigar manufacturer named Markee open-
ed up in my place the first day following
its vacation by the thrifty merchant, but
not for $15 a month.   The merchant, you

see, had increased the value of my property by building a very substantial business house and residence right next to it and some new buildings had gone up across the street and in the adjoining blocks, and Mr. Markee was very glad to pay me $30 a month for a period of one year provided I would add a store front and an additional room in the rear. I told him I never improved. There was the house and lot. He could use the lot for $25 a month and do what he pleased with the house. Under no circumstances would I improve the property.

"Mr. Markee looked at me in amazement.

"'How can you expect to rent the place if you don't keep a decent house on it?" he remarked.

"'Easy enough,' said I. 'If you don't want the property just as it stands, for $25 a month for one year, you don't have to take it.'

"'I know I don't have to take it.' replied Markee; 'but it's the best I can find for my business, only I can't do business in such a shack as that.'

"'Then go ahead,' said I, 'and fix the building just as you want it. I'll rent you the lot for $25 a month and you may do as please with the building.'

"'You are very kind, indeed,' replied Mr. Markee. 'I can do as I please with the building only I can't move it off without you should say so.'

"'O,' I hastily added. 'I mean of course you can make any changes you like.'

"Markee squirmed around a good while, but he had to take his medicine. That is, he calculated that my place offered him a good opportunity to do business and he had to accept my terms or go somewhere else. He concluded to accept my terms.

"'Now,' said Markee, after an agreement between us had been drawn up and the property was his for a year, 'now, if somebody would just come along and build a street car line on this street I believe it would make business hum.'

"The observation of Markee," continued Mr. Bowen, "gave me a cue that has enabled me to amass immense wealth and led to causes that have served to keep Markee's nose to the grindstone from that day to this. I went to my friends and proposed the construction of a street railway on my street and a number of other promising thoroughfares.

"'Takes too much money,' observed Charley Neeld.

"'Not a cent,' I replied.

"'Not a cent less than a million,' said Neeld.

"'It will cost lots of money to build the street car lines,' I explained to Neeld and my friends, 'but it need not come out of our pockets—that's what I mean.'

"'O, I see through it now,' broke in Neeld. 'You would build the line on credit and then sell it for more than it cost to build it, would you?'"

"'No.'

"'Then what?'

"'Gentlemen, listen,' l said to them. 'I have given this subject the most thorough examination, and say to you now that we can build this street car line without a cent of cost to ourselves and keep control of it and the profits in the bargain.'

"'Boys,' Neeld laughed. 'George Archie has got 'em for sure this time. See that strange look in his eye!'

"'Laugh if you want to boys, I will show you that I am right.'

"'I see through his scheme,' Ed Laakman ventured to say. 'He would first borrow a lot of money, then go into bankruptcy and after everything was all over go ahead and build the street car line.'

"'That's it,' said all the boys, shouting.

"'Gentlemen,' I said earnestly, 'listen to me. Let me explain to you how we can build this street car line without a cent of cost to ourselves and thus control it and collect all the profits.'

"After the boys had exchanged sly winks among themselves and Neeld had cautioned them to allow me a chance to explain, I outlined my scheme.

"'You see, boys,' said I, 'under the laws of the land, you can get free franchises. That is, the authorities of Chicago have a legal right to pass an ordinance saying that we shall have the exclusive right to build, maintain and operate a street railway on certain streets in the city. Now isn't that true?'

"'Certainly.'

"'Well, boys, suppose we form a company right here, and call it the Chicago Street Railway company. We will be obliged to incorporate before we can do business as a company. We can send $1 to the secretary of state at Springfield and for that $1 he will issue us a charter, signed by the governor and himself, and with this charter from the state in our possession we can go to the city authorities of Chicago and say: We want to build street car lines on your streets. And we ask them to pass an ordinance granting us exclusive privileges, and they reply to us: Street car lines are just what our people want, and they say to us they will give us rights on certain streets forever.

"'And so they pass an ordinance. That ordinance, gentlemen, provides that the Chicago Street Railway company shall have, possess and enjoy, and its heirs and assigns shall have, possess and enjoy, from and after the passage of this ordinance, all the rights, titles and interests of the franchises herewith granted to the Chicago Street Railway company to construct, operate and maintain street railway tracks and cars upon the following streets, to-wit:'

"'And this ordinance, my friends, after its passage, is duly signed and delivered to us. How much is it worth to us?'

"'Gee whiz!' shouted Neeld. 'Boys, I see it all now. Archie is right.'

"'How much would it be worth to us?' I again asked.

"'A million at least,' exclaimed Neeld, excitedly.

"'That's no joke, either,' said Ed Laakman, who seemed to become interested all at once.

" 'Hold on, boys,' I interrupted. 'Don't get excited, I am not through yet. You can all realize that the moment we should get an ordinance into our hands, signed, sealed and delivered, granting us and our heirs and assigns forever exclusive street car rights upon the very best streets in Chicago we would possess something of great value; and very naturally we would have a meeting and decide what the franchise was worth. Suppose we should fix the value at $2,000,000—and it would be worth it—and decide to put our stock to that amount. Of course we could issue $1,000,000 of stock to ourselves for which, of course, we would not pay anything; but we would place the other $1,000,000 in the market to be sold at par. Well, the stock would sell like hot cakes, and we soon find ourselves with lots of money in our hands, and we at once commence building street car lines. We order street cars, buy mules, build barns and make all the necessary preparations for business. Finally the lines are thoroughly equipped and we find upon investigation that from the sale of $500,000 worth of the $1,000,000 placed on the market we have had much more than enough to pay for all expenses of construction. We put the balance in our pockets and being the officers and directors of the company, on big salaries, we have no difficulty in making it appear at the stockholder's meeting that we have done very well. The other fellows having furnished all the money with which to build the lines, we fix them all right by withdrawing from the market the $50,000 worth of stock remaining unsold and issue them 50 per cent. of it without price, and as they know a good thing when they see it, and especially when they get it, harmony is bound to prevail among all interests.'

"'Wouldn't a transaction such as that be illegal?' Neeld asked.

"'Certainly not. The franchise is our exclusive property. It was signed, sealed and delivered to us. If outside parties want a slice of it they get it only upon our terms and we have a legal right to charge any price we see fit. If people don't want to pay it they can leave it alone. If we sell less than half the stock and realize enough to build the line and still own two-thirds of the stock, that's nobody's business but our own. Certainly it's not illegal. I simply say, however, that in order to make everybody feel good, we make the stockholders who furnished the money to build the lines a present of a lot of stock. We do that because we are in great luck ourselves and we feel so good about it that we make the stockholders happy. Now then, gentlemen, you have my scheme. What do you think of it?'

"'Greatest snap on earth. Nothing like it,' declared Neeld.

"'That's a great head you have Archie,' said Laakman.

"And so they all grew enthusiastic over my scheme and a company was at once formed. They elected me as president, of course, and in due time we were a regularly incorporated street car company. The matter of getting rights of way on several of the principal streets of Chicago was soon disposed of, the council passing an ordinance just as we wanted it, and then all the facts were published in the Gazette and property owners along the proposed street car lines at once put up the price of their property. Values went booming generally and everybody felt that Chicago was the coming great city of the northwest. We put out stock for sale and it was eagerly purchased. All of our expectations were realized. It made us all rich except the stockholders. Of course the stockholders realized a fair return on their investment, but with the rest of us it was different, for we had never invested anything, owned two thirds of the stock, consequently two-thirds of the street car lines and therefore absorbed two-thirds of the profits. As the city grew we asked for rights of way on other streets and secured them without difficulty, repeating our former scheme— i. e., building new lines with the money secured from the sale of stock, keeping the bulk of the issue in our own pockets. I will not detain you with a recital of how we followed up this street car franchise business until we had secured a veritable web of streets in the rapidly growing city and how we finally found ourselves millionaires without working or even investing money. O, how plain it all is—and yet—God forgive the nation!—how legal it all is! How just the church regards it! How equitable the courts decree it!"

V.

Thus I had Mr. Bowen's story of "How to Get Rich Without Working." I confess I was amazed. It seemed incredible that such things could be possible under our boasted Declaration of Independence and under the Stars and Stripes. Yet that was everywhere happening—not only in the United States but throughout the broad land—admitted of no doubt. I had known all along that such conditions existed, but it had never once occurred to me that there was anything wrong in the system. It was in existence when I came into action and of course I accepted it as right. My father had never said it was wrong. I had never heard anyone challenge it. I knew the courts had never assailed it. In fact, it had never occurred to me that there was any question to be raised concerning the land system, which everybody accepted as absolutely just.

But now it was clear to me that there was something radically wrong. The Astors were worth $200,000,000—why? Because of the presence of 4,000,000 people in New York, Brooklyn and Jersey City. The Astors were deriving a great income from thousands of people from an investment of

money secured originally from business
men and workingmen. I could see now
how it was possible to prove that the wealth
claimed by the Astors could be taken from
them. Suppose the 4,000,000 people living in and about New York should emigrate
—what would become of the $200,000,000
wealth of the Astors? From whom could
they derive income? Ah, you say if the
people of New York should emigrate somebody else would take their places. True
enough; but it only goes to prove that the
Astors must depend upon the presence of
population and industry for their fabulous
incomes. They toil not neither do they
spin. They are rent gatherers, dogs in the
manger, who contribute nothing to progress,
but like Captain Kidd of old, demand ran-
som from all the rest of mankind.

"Essington," said Bowen, who evidently
knew I was much impressed with his story,
"what do you think of it? Have I not
told you the truth? Did you ever see it in
print before? And is it not true as the
Holy Book?"

"Yes," I replied, warmly. "The remarkable thing is that the truth is so glar-
ing and that nobody has eyes large enough
to see it. But I want to ask you a few
questions before I go."

"Fire away."

"You said that Markee gave you a cue
to a street car scheme that led to results
that kept his nose to the grindstone from
that day to this. How?"

"Why, don't you see, just as soon as

we built the street car line on the street where he did business property values went up, and consequently rents went up. Markee had to pay more rent for doing business on my lot.   Then, you know, we did not stop at building street car lines. We followed right up, in due time, with gas works.   We secured exclusive rights. Didn't cost a cent to build the works.   We let the stockholders do that.   Of course rents went up when the gas works were completed.   Then the city followed with sewers and better sidewalks, adding great value to our land.   We accordingly increased rents.   Every time any improvements took place Markee of course found himself obliged to pay more rent.   Of course he could have snapped his fingers in my face and left my property, but what good would that have done him ?   I would simply have rented to somebody else and he would simply have paid rent to some other landlord.   Markee was business man enough to understand that, as a landlord, I was as good as he could find, and for that matter he and I were always on the best of terms, and to this day he does not blame me for the high rent, "If I don't pay it somebody else will," he has confessed to me many a time.   Just now there are 12 to 24-story buildings all about Markee's little cigar store.   There is still an old shack on the lot.   I have never put a dime's worth of improvement on it. It is worth $200,000.   I am holding it for $300,000.   Markee is paying me $16,000

a year rent just for the use of the lot.   In
the 25 years he has occupied the place he
has not made $16,000.   Practically all the
money comes to me.   What have I done?
Not a thing.   Not a dollar of my own money did I ever invest.   The hustling people
of Chicago made me rich.   They have
worked and paid my syndicate for the privileges they enjoy.   We secured exclusive
franchises, exclusive privileges, until finally
we were in a position to dictate terms.   All
we need to do now is simply say to the
toilers of Chicago, 'Fish or cut bait.'   You
see, under the law, we are the supreme
rulers.   Of course, the people have a right
to change the law, but they may never do
it.   They seem to like injustice.   They praise
injustice.   The church worships injustice.
Tell them my story, which is the story of
thousands of millionaires, and see if they
bat an eye.   Right in the very face of the
truth of my story they will go right on
praising the Lord for things as they are.
But what other question, Mr. Essington?"

"Only this: Are steam railroads con-
structed after the manner in which you
built the Chicago street railways?"

"I am glad you asked that question.
Yes and no.   There is this difference.   We
secure right of way from town to town and
city to city often without consideration,
many farmers being anxious to have railroads traverse their farms, on the theory
that increased land values result; but where
we must pay for the right of way we often
issue stock for it, and having finally secured

right of way from one end of the line to the other we induce the counties through which surveys were made to vote on the question of one or two or three per cent. tax for from 5 to 20 years in aid of the proposed road.   Ninety per cent. of the counties vote the tax, which generally affords enough money to build and equip this line.   So in, that way we become owners of great railroads, without making any investments, and we make matters warm for the farmer who gave us his land for stock by 'freezing him out;' and we make it warm for everybody else by making them pay exorbitant freight rates.   Don't you see how easy it is to become rich without working?"

"Yes; but there are no such opportunities open for me.   You fellows have gobbled everything."

"Keep your eye open.   You can't tell what may turn up.   The world stands ready to help any man who wants to get rich without working.   The laws everywhere are in his favor.   All those who toil must pay tribute to the man who holds special privilege."

"But as for me," said Mr. Bowen, as I was about to bid him good-bye, "I am in favor of changing the laws.   I want to see the country adopt the single land value tax system.   That will settle the whole question."

www.ingramcontent.com/pod-product-compliance
Lightning Source LLC
Chambersburg PA
CBHW060006230526
45472CB00008B/1973